JAPAN
Pocket Travel Guide

J.B TERRY

Copyright ©2023 by J. B Terry

All rights reserved. No part of his book may be reproduced or used in any manner without written permission of the copyright owner except for the use of quotations in a review.

FIRST EDITION MAR. 2024

MY AUTHOR CENTRAL

More Books from Here

TABLE OF CONTENTS

INTRODUCTION 9
   Why You Need This Pocket Guide: 9
CHAPTER 1 13
   BRIEF OVERVIEW 13
      Brief History 15
      Geography and Climate of Japan 18
CHAPTER 2 21
PLANNING YOUR TRIP 21
      The Best Time to Visit Japan 21
      Visa Requirements for Visiting Japan 25
      Budgeting and Costs for a Trip to Japan . 28
CHAPTER 3 33
   GETTING AROUND 33
      Transportation Overview 33
      Guide to the Japan Rail Pass (JR Pass) ... 38
      Navigating Public Transportation 41

Japan Travel Guide   J.B TERRY

CHAPTER 4 45

   ACCOMMODATION 45

      Types of Accommodation 45

      Booking Tips for Traveling to Japan 50

      Unique Stays in Japan 52

      10 Best Cheap Hotels in Japan 55

      (Their Addresses and Phone Numbers)... 55

CHAPTER 5 66

   CUISINE AND DINING 66

      Japanese Food Culture 66

      Must-Try Dishes 69

      Dining Etiquette 74

CHAPTER 6 78

   EXPLORING TOKYO 78

      Top Attractions 78

      Hidden Gems 84

      Day Trips from Tokyo 87

Japan Travel Guide   J.B TERRY

CHAPTER 7 90

DISCOVERING KYOTO 90

Temples and Shrines 90

Must-See Sights: 90

Hidden Gems: 91

Traditional Culture 93

Kyoto's Culinary Delights 98

CHAPTER 8 102

ADVENTURES IN OSAKA 102

Osaka's Vibrant Scene 102

Street Food Paradise 105

Osaka Castle and Beyond 109

CHAPTER 9 112

CULTURAL EXPERIENCES 112

Tea Ceremony 112

Sumo Wrestling 116

Traditional Festivals 119

CHAPTER 10 124

    SHOPPING AND SOUVENIRS 124

        Popular Shopping Districts.................. 124

        Unique Souvenirs to Buy 127

        Tax-Free Shopping Tips 131

CHAPTER 11 134

    PRACTICAL TIPS AND RESOURCES 134

        Language Basics 134

        Cultural Etiquette 138

        Emergency Contacts 143

CHAPTER12 146

    CONCLUSION 146

    Final Thoughts on Japan 146

        Encouragement for Future Travelers 148

Chapter 13 152

    Bonus section 152

        Itinerary 152

Total Cost for A Trip to Japan 154

Tips for Budget Travel: 156

The City Map 157

Travel Budget Planner 159

Travel Journals 161

.... 161

Japan Travel Guide   **J.B TERRY**

INTRODUCTION

Welcome to this Japan Pocket Travel Guide! This little but well loaded book is like your best friend for exploring Japan. It's filled with helpful tips, cool itineraries, and all the important stuff you need to know. With this guide, you can easily discover the amazing sights and culture of Japan. From busy Tokyo streets to peaceful Kyoto temples, and even the stunning Mount Fuji, this book has got you covered. Lots of travelers have used it and had awesome adventures. Are you ready to start your own incredible journey through Japan?

Why You Need This Pocket Guide:

This Pocket Travel Guide to Japan offers a compact yet comprehensive resource for travelers seeking an unforgettable experience in this vibrant destination. Here are some of the key highlights that make this guide a must-have for anyone planning a trip to Japan:

1. **Concise and Practical:** Designed as a pocket-sized companion, this guide provides essential information in a concise format, making it easy to carry and reference on the go.

2. **Insider Tips:** Discover hidden gems, local secrets, and insider tips that will enhance your Japan experience and help you explore the country like a seasoned traveler.

3. **Top Attractions:** Uncover the top attractions, activities, and must-see places in Japan, ensuring you make the most of your time in this diverse and captivating country.

4. **Cultural Insights:** Gain valuable cultural insights, historical background, and

practical advice to deep yourself in the rich heritage of Japan and connect with its vibrant local culture.

5. **Emergency Preparedness:** Stay informed and prepared for emergencies with essential guidelines on how to handle various situations, ensuring your safety and well-being during your travels.

6. **Local Recommendations:** Benefit from curated recommendations on where to eat, drink, shop, and stay, based on expert insights and traveler reviews, to enjoy the best of Japan's culinary and hospitality offerings.

7. **Practical Information:** Find practical information on visas, transportation, currency, language, and more, to navigate Japan with ease and confidence.

8. **Budget-Friendly Options:** Discover budget-friendly accommodations, dining spots, and activities to make the most of your trip without breaking the bank.

9. **Personalized Itineraries:** Get sample itineraries and customizable suggestions to tailor your trip to your preferences and interests, ensuring a personalized and memorable experience in Japan.

10. **Travel journals and travel budget planners included.**

With its blend of practical advice, local insights, and essential information, the Pocket Travel Guide to Japan is your go-to companion for a seamless, enriching, and unforgettable journey to this amazing country.

CHAPTER 1

BRIEF OVERVIEW

The overview of Japan shows a country that mixes old traditions with new ideas, making it a fascinating place to visit. Japan consists of four primary islands: Honshu, Hokkaido, Kyushu, and Shikoku. These islands have diverse landscapes, from snowy mountains to green forests and beautiful beaches. The weather changes a lot throughout the year because of Japan's different terrains.

Japan has a long history filled with traditions and cultural values. People have lived there for thousands of years, coming from places like China and Korea. According to legend, Japan was founded in 660 B.C. by Emperor Jimmu. This marks the start of a rich history that has shaped Japan's identity.

Over time, Japan has grown through many cultural and political changes. Different periods, like the Jomon, Yayoi, and Kofun periods, brought new ideas and practices to Japan. The Yamato clan, said to be descended from the sun goddess Amaterasu Omikami, ruled Japan for a long time. The Heian period, which happened later, saw the rise of a sophisticated culture in Kyoto. This culture mixed native Shinto beliefs with Buddhism and influenced Japan's art, literature, and way of life.

During other times, like the Kamakura, Muromachi, and Edo periods, Japan experienced feudal rule, samurai warriors, and times of keeping away from the rest of the world. But in 1868, the Meiji Restoration changed everything. Japan modernized quickly and started a democratic government.

Today, Japan is a strong country with a big economy. It's known for its technology, culture, and how it mixes old traditions with new ones. Japan continues to influence the world, showing a society that respects its past while looking toward the future.

Brief History

The history of Japan is like a colorful tapestry woven with ancient stories, cultural shifts, and important events that have shaped the country over thousands of years. From mythical beginnings to the modern age, Japan's history is a fascinating journey through time.

Mythical Origins and Early History

The history of Japan starts with ancient myths, one of which tells the story of Emperor Jimmu founding the nation in 660 B.C. These myths laid the foundation for Japan's unique culture and social order, which evolved over many centuries.

Feudal Japan and the Samurai Era

During the feudal period, powerful samurai warriors ruled Japan under a system called shogunate. This era saw the rise of feudal lords known as daimyo, and the strict code of bushido that guided the samurai's way of life.

Meiji Restoration and Modernization

In 1868, the Meiji Restoration brought significant changes to Japan. Imperial rule was reinstated, Western technologies were adopted, and the country rapidly industrialized, becoming modern and competitive on the global stage.

World War II and Postwar Reconstruction

During World War II, Japan was involved in global conflict and suffered greatly from atomic bombings in Hiroshima and Nagasaki. After the war, Japan worked hard to rebuild, eventually becoming a strong economic force in the world.

Contemporary Japan and Global Influence

Today, Japan is known for its technology, culture, and peaceful society. It has a big impact on the world in areas like technology, art, food, and entertainment, showing how it blends tradition with modern life.

Looking at Japan's history from ancient times to now shows the strength, flexibility, and creativity of its people. The diverse stories of Japan's past continue to intrigue and inspire people worldwide, making it a fascinating subject to explore and learn about.

Geography and Climate of Japan

Geography

Japan is a collection of islands located in the Pacific Ocean, consisting of four main islands: Honshu, Hokkaido, Kyushu, and Shikoku, along with many smaller ones. The country covers approximately 378,000 square kilometers, which puts it in the same size category as countries like Germany, Finland, Vietnam, or Malaysia. Its coastline varies, with some areas having long sandy beaches while others feature rugged cliffs. Japan's terrain is marked by mountains, volcanoes, and valleys, with about 73% of its land being mountainous. Mount Fuji, standing at 3,776 meters, is the tallest peak and a symbol of Japan.

Climate

Japan's climate is influenced by its location, ocean currents, and winds. The country is divided into six main climate zones, each with its own characteristics:

- **Hokkaido:** Experiences a humid continental climate with cold winters, cool summers, and heavy snowfall.

- **Sea of Japan region:** Receives heavy snow in winter due to northwest winds, while summers are less rainy but can be very hot.

- **Central Highland:** Has an inland climate with big temperature differences between seasons and lower rainfall.

- **Seto Inland Sea region:** Enjoys a mild climate with lots of sunny days because of mountains.

- **Pacific Ocean side:** Has milder winters and sunnier conditions than the Sea of Japan side, with hot summers and heavy rainfall.

- **Ryukyu Islands:** Located in the south, they have a humid subtropical climate with warm winters, hot summers, and high rainfall influenced by the rainy season and typhoons.

Japan's climate is complex, with significant differences between its west and east coasts due to mountains and oceanic influences. The country experiences four distinct seasons, each offering its own climate experience: winter, spring, summer, and autumn. Overall, Japan's geography and climate contribute to its natural beauty and diverse ecosystems, making it a fascinating destination for travelers and nature lovers.

CHAPTER 2

PLANNING YOUR TRIP

The Best Time to Visit Japan

When to visit Japan depends on what you like and what you want to do, as each season offers different experiences across the country. Below is a breakdown of the best times to visit Japan based on different factors:

Best Times for Smaller Crowds:

- **High Season:** March to May and September to November are popular times with nice weather and lots of festivals.

- **Shoulder Seasons:** June to August and December are less crowded, so it's a good time to explore without too many tourists around.

- **Low Season:** January to March is quieter, great for sightseeing and enjoying snow sports and hot springs.

Best Times for Good Weather:

- **March to May and September to November:** These times usually have the best weather, perfect for outdoor activities and sightseeing.

Best Time for Cherry Blossoms:

- Cherry blossoms bloom from late March to early April in places like Kyoto and Tokyo. In northern cities like Sapporo, they might bloom later, around May.

Best Times for Food Lovers:

- Japan has delicious food all year round, with each season offering different specialties. For example, summer has cool sōmen noodles and shaved ice, while autumn brings matsutake mushrooms and sweet potatoes.

Worst Times to Visit:

- **Rainy Season:** Early June to mid-July is rainy and humid in most of Japan.

- **Golden Week:** End of April to early May is busy and expensive because it's a popular time for travel.

Additional Tips:

- **May and October:** These months are great for visiting Japan because the weather is nice, there are fewer tourists, and prices are lower.

- **Southern Japan:** April and October are good times to visit because it's warm but not too crowded.

- **Tokyo and Kyoto:** Visit Tokyo in April for mild weather and fewer crowds, and go to Kyoto between October and March to avoid the busiest times.

In conclusion, the best time to visit Japan depends on what you're looking for, whether it's cherry blossoms, good weather, or fewer crowds. Planning your trip around these factors can make your experience in Japan even better.

Visa Requirements for Visiting Japan

The visa requirements for visiting Japan depend on why you're going and where you're from. Below is a summary of the main things you need to know:

Short-Term Visit (Tourism/Business/Conference/Study):

- You'll need a valid passport with enough blank pages, a 2"x 2" photo, and a U.S. visa if you're from the U.S.

- You also need proof of residency, a travel itinerary, flight details, and a bank statement.

- If you're going for business, you'll need an invitation letter from the company you're visiting, and a letter from your own company.

- For a conference, you'll need an invitation letter and details about the conference.

- If you're visiting family or friends, you'll need an invitation from them, their ID, and possibly more documents if they're covering your expenses.

eVISA System (Electronic Visa):

- The JAPAN eVISA system lets you apply online for short visits for tourism.

- It's available for residents of certain countries, except those who don't need short-term visas.

- You can get a single-entry visa for up to 90 days for tourism.

- You have to travel to Japan by plane and might need to go for an interview at a Japanese office abroad.

- Only people with ordinary passports can use the JAPAN eVISA system.

General Visa Application Procedures:

- Regular visa applications take about 5 business days to process.

- It's best to apply about 1.5 months before you plan to leave.

- You'll need your passport, a visa application form, your travel plans, and other documents depending on why you're going.

When you're planning a trip to Japan, make sure to check the visa requirements for your nationality and why you're visiting. Follow the guidelines from Japanese authorities to make sure your visa application goes smoothly.

Budgeting and Costs for a Trip to Japan

When planning a trip to Japan, it's important to budget for various expenses like accommodation, food, transportation, and sightseeing. Below is a breakdown of costs based on different budget ranges:

Accommodation Costs:

- *Low Budget:* Dormitories and hostels are affordable, typically charging below 5,000 yen per night per person.

- *Medium Budget:* Single rooms range from 6,000 to 12,000 yen per night, while double rooms range from 8,000 to 15,000 yen per night.

- *High Budget:* Better business hotels start around 12,000 yen per person per night, and staying at a ryokan with meals included can cost between 15,000 and 30,000 yen per person per night.

Food Costs:

- *Low Budget:* Convenience stores and fast-food restaurants offer breakfast options for around 500 yen per day.

- *Medium Budget:* Coffee shops and some restaurants provide breakfast sets for around 500 to 1,000 yen per day.

- *High Budget:* Hotel breakfasts and breakfast buffets can cost more than 1,000 yen per day.

Lunch Costs:

- *Low Budget:* Inexpensive lunch boxes from convenience stores and fast-food restaurants cost around 500 to 800 yen per day.

- *Medium Budget:* Lunch set specials at various restaurants are available for around 800 to 1,500 yen per day.

- *High Budget:* Dining at better restaurants for lunch typically costs between 1,500 and 3,000 yen per day.

Dinner Costs:

- *Low Budget:* Convenience stores offer ready-to-eat meals for 500 to 1,000 yen per day.

- *Medium Budget:* Meals at conventional restaurants range from 1,000 to 2,500 yen per day.

- *High Budget:* Dining at upper-class restaurants specializing in sushi, French cuisine, or other specialties can cost 2,500 yen upwards per day.

Sightseeing Costs:

- *Low Budget:* Many shrines and some temples in Japan do not charge admission fees.

- *Medium Budget:* Admission to famous temples typically costs between 300 and

1,000 yen, while museums and castles charge about 500-1,500 yen per person.

- *High Budget:* Some museums and attractions may charge between 1,500 and 3,000 yen per person.

In conclusion, budgeting for a trip to Japan involves considering accommodation, food, transportation, and sightseeing costs. There are options available for travelers across different budget ranges, and by planning and making informed choices, visitors can enjoy Japan while managing their expenses effectively.

CHAPTER 3

GETTING AROUND

Transportation Overview

Japan provides a seamless and efficient transportation network, offering various choices to suit different preferences and budgets. Below is an overview of the transportation options available:

Japan Rail Pass (JR Pass):

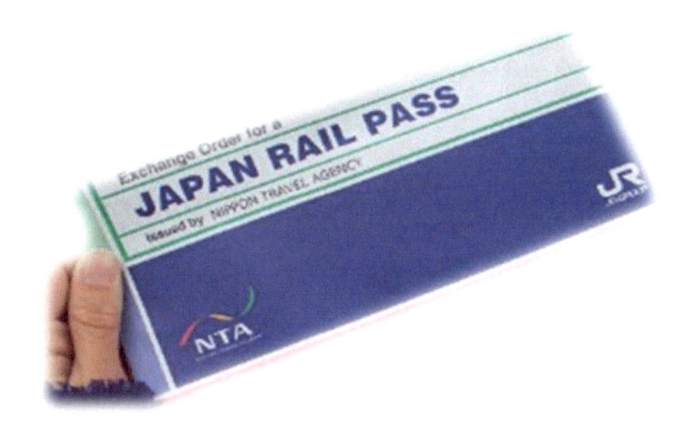

- The Japan Rail Pass is a popular choice for foreign visitors, giving access to almost all Japan Rail trains, including bullet trains.

- It comes in Ordinary and Green (first-class) types, with different prices and seat reservation options.

- It's recommended to buy before arriving in Japan for convenience and cost-effectiveness.

Subway Passes in Tokyo:

- 24/48/72-hour subway passes in Tokyo allow access to all Tokyo Metro and Toei Subway lines.

- Ideal for travelers staying in Tokyo who want to explore the city efficiently.

- It's best to buy these passes before arrival because they're not sold in specific prefectures.

Domestic Flights:

- Domestic flights are convenient for longer distances within Japan.

- Airlines like JAL offer the Japan Explorer Pass, providing discounted rates for flights to various destinations, including Okinawa and scenic spots.

Bicycles:

- Bicycles offer a unique way to explore Japan, especially in cities and rural areas.

- Many tourist offices provide free or low-cost bicycle rental services, allowing travelers to explore rural Japan.

Local Buses:

- Local buses are essential for rural travel and within cities like Kyoto.

- Ticket systems vary, and English information may be limited outside tourist areas.

- Prepaid cards like Suica or Pasmo are handy for bus travel.

Trains:

- Japan's rail network, including the Shinkansen (bullet trains), is modern and efficient, making trains the preferred mode of transportation.

- The Japan Rail Pass offers unlimited train travel within Japan for a set number of days, providing flexibility and convenience.

In conclusion, Japan offers a diverse range of transportation options, from high-speed trains to local buses and bicycles, catering to different travel needs and preferences. Understanding these options can help visitors navigate Japan efficiently and make the most of their travel experience in this fascinating country.

Guide to the Japan Rail Pass (JR Pass)

Eligibility for Use:

- The Japan Rail Pass is only for foreign tourists visiting Japan under the entry status of "temporary visitor."

- To use it, visitors must have a stamp or sticker in their passport indicating "Temporary Visitor" status upon entry into Japan.

- The pass cannot be used by individuals under other official statuses like "Trainee" or "Reentry Permit."

Conditions for Use:

- The pass is personal and can only be used by the person whose passport information is registered to it.

- Passengers must carry their passport at all times and be ready to show it when asked by station staff.

- It's valid for ordinary cars on all Japan Railways (JR Line) Shinkansen "bullet trains" and other specified modes of transportation.

Validity and Usage:

- The Japan Rail Pass comes in 7-, 14-, and 21-day options, with consecutive days of use, not just travel days.

- Holders can use various JR trains, including the shinkansen, local trains, and metro services in Tokyo, Kyoto, and Osaka.

- It also covers other transportation like JR Buses, JR Ferry, Monorails, and airport transfers.

How to Use the JR Pass:

- Travelers buy the pass and get an exchange voucher by mail, which they must validate and exchange for the actual pass in Japan.

- The exchange must be done within 90 days of purchase at a JR Exchange Office, usually found at airports and main train stations.

- When exchanging, travelers fill out a form, show their passport, and pick a start date for the pass.

In summary, the Japan Rail Pass is a great option for foreign tourists visiting Japan, offering unlimited access to JR trains, including the famous shinkansen, and other transportation services. Knowing the eligibility, conditions, and usage guidelines is important for a smooth and budget-friendly travel experience in Japan.

Navigating Public Transportation

Navigating public transportation in Japan involves using a well-organized and efficient system that includes trains, subways, buses, taxis, and even domestic flights. Some key points to consider are:

Train and Subway System:

- Japan's public transportation heavily relies on trains and subways, especially in major cities like Tokyo.

- Trains are clean, punctual, and operate from early morning till late at night, making them a convenient way to travel within and between cities.

- Signs in English at train stations and English-language maps make it easier for foreigners to navigate the system.

IC Cards (Prepaid Cards):

- Prepaid IC cards like Suica or PASMO are essential for using public transportation in Japan.

- These cards can be used for trains, buses, subways, some taxis, stores, restaurants, vending machines, and coin lockers.

- IC cards offer convenience by allowing seamless travel across different regions in Japan.

Shinkansen (Bullet Train) and Domestic Flights:

- For long-distance travel within Japan, options include the high-speed Shinkansen bullet train and domestic flights.

- The Shinkansen is known for its speed, comfort, and efficiency in connecting various parts of the country.

Taxis and Buses:

- Taxis are easily available in cities and can be hailed from train stations or streets.

- Buses run along major roads and provide an alternative mode of transport within cities and to remote areas.

Additional Tips:

- It's advisable to have a passport or Japanese government-issued ID when using public transportation as a foreign resident or visitor.

- Apps are available for easily calling taxis in Japan, though services like Uber are not as common.

- Understanding how to use IC cards, purchase tickets at stations, transfer between different modes of transport, and listen for announcements on buses are essential for smooth navigation.

In conclusion, Japan's public transportation system offers a reliable, clean, and efficient way to travel within the country. By familiarizing yourself with the various modes of transport available and utilizing tools like IC cards and apps for convenience, navigating public transport in Japan can be a seamless experience for both residents and visitors alike.

CHAPTER 4

ACCOMMODATION

Types of Accommodation

Hotels:

- Hotels in Japan range from luxury to more economical options, catering to diverse traveler preferences and budgets.

- They offer exceptional service, cleanliness, and amenities like restaurants, gyms, and Wi-Fi.

- Conveniently located near public transportation hubs or tourist areas, hotels provide a comfortable and reliable stay.

Ryokan (Traditional Inns):

- Ryokan offers a unique and immersive experience into Japan's rich cultural heritage.

- These traditional inns provide exceptional hospitality, serene ambiance, and attention to detail.

- Often located near natural hot springs or picturesque landscapes, ryokan offer tatami-mat rooms, futons, communal baths (onsen), and kaiseki meals.

Capsule Hotels:

- Capsule hotels are a modern concept where small capsules replace traditional hotel rooms.

- These affordable accommodations feature basic amenities like a bed, TV, and Wi-Fi.

- Popular among travelers seeking a unique and budget-friendly stay.

Minshuku (B&B):

- Minshuku are traditional Japanese guesthouses located in rural areas, offering an authentic and immersive experience.

- Family-run establishments with tatami mat rooms, shared bathrooms, and locally sourced meals.

- Ideal for travelers looking to experience Japanese culture and hospitality in a down-to-earth setting.

Business Hotels:

- Business hotels are smaller and more affordable versions of Western-style hotels.

- Typically located near train stations, they offer basic amenities suitable for business travelers or budget-conscious tourists.

- Prices range from ¥5,000 to ¥13,000 per night.

Minpaku (Private Lodging):

- Private homes rented out to travelers for short or long-term stays.

- Refurbished countryside homes offering an authentic experience at an affordable price.

- A more immersive option compared to traditional hotels.

Temple Lodging (Shukubo):

- A unique accommodation experience offered by Buddhist temples in Japan.

- Provides travelers with the opportunity to experience Japanese Buddhist culture through meditation sessions, vegetarian meals, and temple activities.

- A peaceful and serene retreat for off-the-beaten-path travelers.

These diverse accommodation options in Japan cater to various preferences, budgets, and experiences, ensuring that travelers can find the perfect place to stay during their visit to the Land of the Rising Sun.

Booking Tips for Traveling to Japan

1. Itinerary Planning:

- Plan your itinerary well in advance to determine the duration of your stay in each place and the activities you want to do.

- Consider any construction, closures, or holidays that may affect your plans and bookings.

2. Passport and Visa:

- Ensure you have a valid passport to enter Japan, and check if your country requires a visa for entry.

- Make photocopies of your passport, IDs, credit, and debit cards as a precaution.

3. Accommodation Reservations:

- Book your accommodations, whether hotels or Airbnbs, ahead of time, especially if you prefer specific locations or amenities.

- Check the room size and proximity to train stations for convenience during your stay.

4. **Currency Exchange:**

- Convert some money to Japanese Yen before your trip, as cash is widely used in Japan, and many places may only accept cash payments.

- Compare exchange rates and options to get the best deal on currency exchange.

5. **Pocket Wi-Fi or SIM Card:**

- Stay connected by renting a pocket Wi-Fi or getting a SIM card for your phone.

- Reserve your pocket Wi-Fi or SIM card in advance to ensure connectivity upon arrival in Japan.

By following these booking tips, you can streamline your travel preparations, ensure a smooth experience in Japan, and make the most of your trip without any last-minute hassles.

Unique Stays in Japan

1. **Hirado Castle Stay:**

- Experience a stay in the historic Hirado Castle, built in 1559. Enjoy activities like tea ceremonies, trying on traditional clothing, and outdoor adventures like horseback riding.

2. **Kurabito Stay:**

- Stay at a 300-year-old sake brewery in Saku, Nagano Prefecture. You can even learn how to brew sake and explore the old brewery's architecture.

3. **Blue Train Taragi:**

- Spend a night in a retired JR Sleeper Train near Taragi Station in Kumamoto Prefecture.

These unique lodgings are made from converted passenger cars and offer a special overnight experience.

4. **Nipponia Sawara Merchant Town Hotel:**

- Stay in a luxury hotel in Sawara, a historic town from the Edo period. You'll get to experience traditional Japanese architecture and stay in beautifully restored historic buildings.

5. **Funuya Accommodation:**

- Enjoy a getaway in a traditional boathouse in Ine waterfront, Kyoto Prefecture. Choose from a selection of charming boathouse hideaways and enjoy activities like fishing, kayaking, and guided tours.

6. **The Ninja Mansion:**

- Rent a historic home in a rural village in Toyota, renovated into a unique rental accommodation. Surrounded by lovely gardens, this place offers a one-of-a-kind experience.

7. **Koyasan Temple Lodgings:**

- Experience the peaceful atmosphere of a monk-style bed and breakfast in Koyasan. Over 50 temples offer overnight stays where you can join in temple activities and learn about Buddhist culture.

These unique accommodations in Japan provide a chance to immerse yourself in the country's history, culture, and traditions while enjoying a memorable and special place to stay.

10 Best Cheap Hotels in Japan

(Their Addresses and Phone Numbers)

Below are the top 10 best affordable hotels in Japan. From bustling city centers to serene countryside retreats, these budget-friendly accommodations offer comfort and convenience without breaking the bank. Each hotel comes with its address, contact phone number, and their pictures, ensuring a memorable stay at an unbeatable price.

However, you're are advised to cross-check the phone numbers as they may have changed over time.

1. Tobu Hotel Levant Tokyo

FACILITIES:

- 24-hour check-in
- 24-hour front desk
- Shuttle bus service

Address:

1-2-2 Kinshi, Sumida 130-0013 Tokyo Prefecture

Phone:

03-5611-5511

ABOUT

TOBU HOTEL LEVANT TOKYO offers an ideal location and proximity. Guests can enjoy being in the heart of the tourist area near TOKYO SKYTREE®, Asakusa, and shopping centers. The hotel is conveniently located just 300m from Kinshicho Station. Some rooms and restaurants offer a wonderful view of TOKYO SKYTREE®, adding to the romantic atmosphere. Additionally, guests benefit from superb accessibility to major attractions, including shuttle buses to Tokyo Disneyland® and direct airport limousines to Haneda and Narita International Airport

2. Hotel Brighton City Osaka Kitahama

FACILITIES:

- Bath/shower
- Flatscreen TV
- Taxi service

Address:

1-1 Fushimimachi, Chuo, Osaka 541-0044 Osaka Prefecture

Phone: +81 6-6223-7771.

ABOUT:

Hotel Brighton City Osaka Kitahama is an excellent choice for travelers visiting Osaka, offering a trendy environment with helpful amenities to enhance your stay. The rooms feature flat-screen TVs, air conditioning, and free WiFi for your convenience. Guests can enjoy a 24-hour front desk, baggage storage, and an on-site restaurant. With popular landmarks like Hep Five Ferris Wheel and Shinsaibashi nearby, guests can easily explore Osaka's attractions. If you enjoy steakhouses, several are within reach. Don't miss out on visiting Osaka Castle and Tenjimbashisuji Shopping Street, both within walking distance. Enjoy your stay in Osaka!

3. Hotel Palm Royal Naha Kokusai

FACILITIES:

- **Bath/shower**

Address:

3-9-10 Makishi, Naha 900-0013 Okinawa Prefecture

Phone:

009 81 98-865-5551

ABOUT

Located in the heart of NAHA on Kokusai Street, the hotel offers easy access to Naha's main streets and Makishi Station. Guests can enjoy the newly opened outdoor pool and poolside bar in summer 2019. In 2018, a new building equipped with a spa and art gallery in the RAM Tower corridors was opened, all non-smoking for their convenience.

4. Sakura Terrace The Gallery

FACILITIES:

- 24-hour front desk
- **Taxi service**
- **Flatscreen**

Address:

39 Kamitonodacho, Higashikujo ,Minami-ku, Kyoto 601-8002 Kyoto Prefecture

Phone:

+81-75-672-0002.

ABOUT

To ensure a tranquil atmosphere for every guest and due to the hotel's design, children under 12 years old cannot stay. Children aged 13 and above will be counted as 1 adult. Additionally, to maintain a serene environment, the hotel does not accept group reservations exceeding 3 rooms.

5. Park Hotel Tokyo

FACILITIES:

- Bath/shower
- Flatscreen tv
- 24-hour check-in

Address:

1-7-1 Higashi Shimbashi Shiodome Media Tower, Minato 105-7227 Tokyo Prefecture

Phone:

+81-3-6252-1111

ABOUT

Park Hotel Tokyo, located in the Shiodome Media Tower since 2003, offers a stunning view of the city from its lobby on the 25th floor. With 270 guest rooms from the 26th to 34th floors, the hotel introduced a new concept in 2013, focusing on Japanese beauty. Currently, room decorations on the 31st floor are underway to enhance guests' experience further.

6. JR Kyushu Hotel Blossom Shinjuku

FACILITIES:

- **Bath/shower**
- **Flatscreen TV**
- **24-hour check-in**

Address:

2-6-2, Yoyogi, Shibuya 460-0003 Tokyo Prefecture

Phone:

+81-3-5333-8687

ABOUT

For travelers in Shinjuku, JR Kyushu Hotel Blossom Shinjuku offers a charming environment and easy access to restaurants and attractions. Guest rooms include amenities like flat-screen TVs and free WiFi. Enjoy on-site dining and 24-hour service. Explore nearby landmarks such as Meiji Jingu Shrine and Yoyogi Park. Whether for business or pleasure, JR Kyushu Hotel Blossom Shinjuku ensures a memorable stay in Shinjuku and Shibuya.

Japan Travel Guide   J.B TERRY

7. Hotel Sunroute Plaza Shinjuku

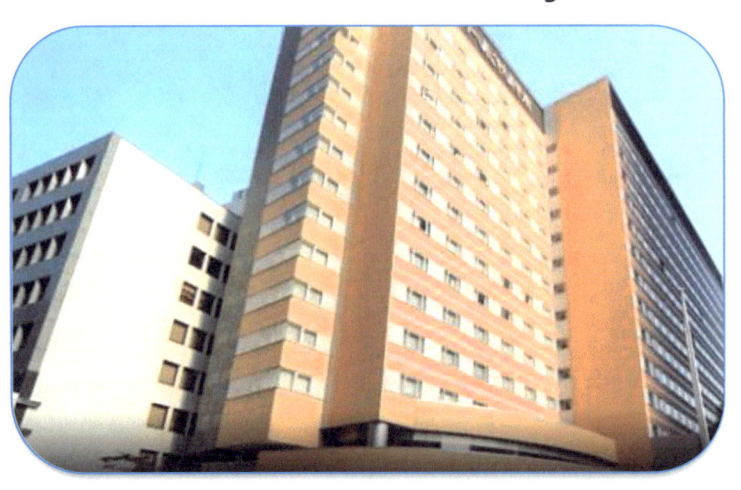

FACILITIES:

- **Complimentary toiletries**
- **Flatscreen TV**
- **Taxi service**
- **Hair dryer**

Address:

2-3-1, Yoyogi, Shibuya 151-0053 Tokyo Prefecture

Phone:

+81 3-3375-3211

ABOUT

Hotel Sunroute Plaza Shinjuku is a stylish hotel located in Tokyo's bustling Shinjuku business district. Renovated in 2007, its contemporary guestrooms cater to both business and leisure travelers. With competitive pricing and various room options, guests enjoy a convenient stay near corporate offices and public transportation. Indulge in Italian cuisine at Villazza restaurant and unwind at Bar Ku Kon.

8. Daiwa Roynet Hotel Ginza Premier

FACILITIES:

- 24-hour front desk
- Flatscreen TV
- Complimentary toiletries
- Hair dryer

Address:

1-13-15, Ginza, Chuo 104-0061 Tokyo Prefecture

Phone:

81-3-5159-1380,

ABOUT

Daiwa Royent Hotel GINZA PREMIER opened on December 1st, 2015, situated in Tokyo's Ginza district. It's a 40-minute subway and walking distance from Haneda International Airport.

9. Richmond Hotel Fukuoka Tenjin

FACILITIES:

- Complimentary toiletries
- Flatscreen TV
- Taxi service
- Hair dryer

Address:

1-13-15, Ginza, Chuo 104-0061 Tokyo Prefecture

Phone:

+81-92-717-2477

+81 92-739-2055

ABOUT

Daiwa Royent Hotel GINZA PREMIER opened on December 1st, 2015, located in Tokyo's Ginza district. It is a 40-minute subway and walk from Haneda International Airport.

10. Super Hotel Premier Tokyo Station

FACILITIES:

- Complimentary toiletries
- Flatscreen TV
- Taxi service
- Hair dryer

Address:

22-2-7, Yaesu, Chuo 104-0028 Tokyo Prefecture

Phone:

+81 3-3241-9000

03-3241-9000

ABOUT

This hotel's name will change to "Superhotel Premier Tokyo Station Yaesu Chuo-guchi" starting from April 1st. This change reflects their commitment to improvement, and they sincerely appreciate your continued support. Thank you.

CHAPTER 5

CUISINE AND DINING

Japanese Food Culture

Japanese food culture is deeply rooted in tradition and etiquette, reflecting a profound respect for culinary artistry and dining customs. Here are some key insights regarding Japanese food culture:

Significance of Dishes: Japanese chefs pay close attention to detail when selecting colors and patterns for dishes. Plates and bowls are often seasonal, hand-painted, and historically significant. This attention to detail enhances the dining experience and emphasizes the importance of presentation in Japanese cuisine.

Table Manners: Japanese dining etiquette emphasizes respect and appreciation for food. It is important to observe table manners, such as not sticking chopsticks upright in rice or laying them across bowls of noodles. Proper chopstick handling and using chopstick holders or folded napkins show respect for the meal and fellow diners.

Appreciation and Gratitude: The Japanese tradition of expressing gratitude through phrases like "itadakimasu" before meals signifies a deep appreciation for the food, chefs, ingredients, and all those involved in creating the culinary experience. This cultural practice highlights the reverence for food as an essential aspect of Japanese life.

Food Presentation: Presentation is crucial in Japanese cuisine, with chefs focusing on artistic displays that enhance the dining experience. Every element, from the shape of food to the color and texture of ingredients, contributes to creating a visually appealing meal that reflects the chef's skill and storytelling ability.

Culinary Traditions: Traditional Japanese cuisine, known as "washoku," revolves around seasonality and uses locally sourced fresh ingredients prepared with special techniques and utensils. Washoku is not only about food but also an art form that appreciates seasonal offerings and connects with nature through culinary practices.

Japanese food culture embodies a harmonious blend of tradition, artistry, respect, and appreciation for nature's bounty. Dining in

Japan offers a unique and enriching experience that goes beyond mere sustenance.

Must-Try Dishes

Japanese food has a lot more to offer than just sushi and sashimi. Below is a list of dishes you should try to explore the diverse flavors of Japanese cuisine:

1. Sushi and Sashimi:

Sushi is raw fish served on rice seasoned lightly with vinegar, offering a variety of flavors and textures like uni (sea urchin roe) and amaebi (sweet shrimp). Sashimi is thinly sliced raw fish or meat. Both are considered art forms in Japanese cuisine.

2. Ramen:

Ramen consists of egg noodles in a salty broth and is a popular late-night meal in Japan. It comes in various styles like tonkotsu (pork bone), miso, soy sauce, and salt, each offering a unique taste experience.

3. Unagi:

Unagi is river eel grilled over charcoal and glazed with a sweet barbecue sauce. It is believed to be the perfect antidote to Japan's hot summers and is a delicacy with a traditional approach in its preparation.

4. Tempura:

Tempura is a light and fluffy deep-fried dish originating from Japan, where seafood and vegetables are coated in batter and fried in sesame oil. It is known for its attention to detail and Japanese ingredients.

5. Miso Soup:

Miso soup features a stock broth base called "dashi," made from seaweed and smoked fish, mixed with miso paste, tofu, spring onions, vegetables, or seafood. It is customary to lift the bowl to drink the soup and use chopsticks for solid pieces.

6. Okonomiyaki:

Okonomiyaki is a savory pancake made with flour, eggs, shredded cabbage, meat or seafood, topped with various condiments like mayonnaise, bonito flakes, and seaweed powder.

7. Gyoza:

Gyoza are Japanese dumplings filled with ground meat and vegetables, wrapped in thin dough and pan-fried until crispy.

It is typical for them to be served as an appetizer or side dish.

8. Soba:

Soba noodles are made from buckwheat flour and can be enjoyed cold with dipping sauce or hot in broth. They are popular across Japan and come in various varieties depending on the region and season.

These dishes represent a diverse range of flavors, textures, and culinary traditions that showcase the richness of Japanese cuisine.

Dining Etiquette

Japanese dining etiquette, also known as washoku etiquette, puts a strong emphasis on respecting both the food and the host. Here's a rundown of essential etiquette points to ensure a smooth and enjoyable dining experience in Japan:

Before the Meal:

Greetings: When you arrive at a restaurant, greet the staff with a polite bow and wait to be seated.

Using Chopsticks:

Proper Handling:

Hold the bottom chopstick with your non-dominant hand and the top one with your dominant hand, using the rest provided. Avoid rubbing chopsticks together or pointing them at others.

Passing Food: Use serving chopsticks to transfer food from shared plates. Don't use your personal chopsticks for this.

Table Manners:

Itadakimasu!: Before you start eating, say "itadakimasu" to express gratitude for the meal.

Slurping Noodles: It's okay to slurp noodles; it's even encouraged as it enhances their flavor and texture.

Eating Pace: Take moderate bites and chew thoroughly. Avoid talking with your mouth full.

General Etiquette:

Keeping Things Clean: Use a wet napkin provided at the start to clean your hands and face.

No Tipping: Tipping isn't usual in Japan; the bill often includes a service charge.

Paying the Bill: If the bill is on the table, take it to the cashier. If unsure, ask your host for help.

Finishing the Meal:

Gochisosamadeshita!: When done eating, say "gochisosamadeshita" to show gratitude.

Additional Tips:

Shoes Off: In many restaurants, especially traditional ones, remove your shoes before entering. You'll get slippers to wear.

Chopstick Use: If you can't use chopsticks, ask for a fork and knife.

Loud Noise: Keep your voice down while eating; loud talking can disrupt others.

Blowing Your Nose: If you need to blow your nose, leave the table politely.

Following these simple etiquette rules ensures a respectful and enjoyable dining experience in Japan, showing your appreciation for the food and culture.

CHAPTER 6

EXPLORING TOKYO

Top Attractions

Tokyo, Japan's capital, is a dynamic metropolis that seamlessly blends ancient tradition with futuristic innovation. From towering skyscrapers and neon-lit streets to serene temples and tranquil gardens, Tokyo offers a captivating experience for every visitor. Here are some of the top attractions you can't miss:

1. Senso-ji Temple:

Located in Asakusa, Senso-ji Temple is famous for its stunning Kaminarimon Gate and Nakamise Dori shopping street. It's a must-visit destination to delve into Japan's rich history and cultural heritage.

2. Meiji Jingu Shrine:

Nestled near JR Harajuku Station, Meiji Jingu Shrine offers a serene escape in a forested area. Built to honor Emperor Meiji and Empress Shoken, it provides visitors with a peaceful sanctuary away from the city's hustle and bustle.

3. Hamarikyu Gardens:

Offering a tranquil oasis in Tokyo, Hamarikyu Gardens reflect the city's Edo-era past. Visitors can unwind in these beautiful gardens and learn about the historical activities that once took place there.

4. Tokyo Tower:

Completed in 1958, Tokyo Tower provides breathtaking panoramic views of the city from its observation decks. It's a prominent landmark near districts like Roppongi and Toranomon, offering visitors a bird's eye perspective of Tokyo's expansive skyline.

5. Shinjuku Gyoen National Garden:

Spanning vast expanses, Shinjuku Gyoen offers a serene escape within Tokyo's urban heart. Visitors can wander through meticulously landscaped gardens, admire seasonal blooms, and bask in the tranquil atmosphere.

6. Imperial Palace:

Surrounded by lush gardens and moats, the Tokyo Imperial Palace is a significant historical site. While the inner grounds are not accessible to the public, visitors can explore the outer gardens and marvel at the grandeur of the palace complex.

7. Shibuya Crossing:

Known as one of the world's busiest pedestrian crossings, Shibuya Crossing provides a unique and bustling experience in Tokyo. Visitors can witness the organized chaos as crowds of people cross the street from multiple directions.

Ginza District: Renowned as Tokyo's upscale shopping and dining hub, Ginza boasts luxury boutiques, department stores, and fine dining establishments. Exploring the chic streets of Ginza offers visitors a taste of Tokyo's sophisticated side.

These top attractions in Tokyo offer a diverse range of experiences, from cultural immersion at historic sites to modern marvels and bustling cityscapes, providing visitors with a comprehensive glimpse into the vibrant tapestry of Tokyo's attractions.

Hidden Gems

Tokyo holds hidden treasures beyond its famous attractions and bright lights. These lesser-known spots offer a glimpse into the city's local culture and offbeat charm. Below are some hidden gems to add to your Tokyo adventure:

Yanaka Ginza: Take a stroll through the quaint alleys of Yanaka Ginza, a traditional shopping street offering local goods and delicious street food.

Gotokuji Temple: Known as the "Cat Temple," Gotokuji Temple is adorned with hundreds of beckoning cat statues, perfect for cat lovers seeking good luck.

Setagaya Seiroen (Little Venice): Discover the tranquility of "Little Venice" in Setagaya Seiroen, where picturesque canals and weeping willows create a romantic atmosphere.

Hara Museum of Contemporary Art: Escape the crowds and explore modern art at the Hara Museum, showcasing postwar Japanese art and international avant-garde movements.

Meguro Parasitological Museum: Delve into the fascinating world of parasites at this quirky museum, featuring interactive exhibits and real specimens.

Nakano Broadway: Anime and manga enthusiasts will love Nakano Broadway, a multi-story complex filled with shops dedicated to geek culture.

Kichijoji: Experience the vibrant local scene of Kichijoji, with its quirky cafes, independent shops, and the scenic Inokashira Park.

Shinjuku Golden Gai:

Dive into the lively atmosphere of Shinjuku Golden Gai, an alleyway lined with cozy bars offering a unique pub experience.

Tokyo Tower: Ascend Tokyo Tower for panoramic views of the city from a historical landmark.

These hidden gems offer a different perspective of Tokyo, away from the usual tourist spots.

Embrace the opportunity to explore and uncover the city's unique charm.

Day Trips from Tokyo

Tokyo, a bustling city, is a great starting point to explore nearby destinations in Japan. Thanks to its efficient transportation system, you can easily take day trips to discover various cultural experiences, historical sites, and beautiful scenery. Below are some popular options:

Kamakura: This historic city was once Japan's political capital. Explore its rich heritage by visiting the Great Buddha of Kamakura, a huge bronze statue, and Tsurugaoka Hachiman-gu, an important Shinto shrine.

Hakone: If you want to escape the city, Hakone is perfect. It's known for its hot springs, scenic mountains, and Lake Ashi. You can relax in the hot springs, take a cable car ride up Mount Hakone, or enjoy a boat ride on the lake.

Nikko: Nikko is a UNESCO World Heritage Site nestled in the mountains. Explore Toshogu Shrine, a beautifully decorated Shinto shrine, and Rinnoji Temple, known for its Three Monkeys statue.

Kawagoe: Known as "Little Edo," Kawagoe offers a glimpse into Japan's past with its traditional storehouses and Candy Alley, where you can find delicious treats.

Yokohama: Experience the lively atmosphere of Yokohama, a port city with a mix of Japanese and Western influences. Visit the Chinatown or explore the modern Minato Mirai area with its skyscrapers and harbor views.

Mount Takao:

For nature lovers, Mount Takao is a great choice. Hike the scenic trails, enjoy panoramic views from the summit, and relax in a natural hot spring at the top.

No matter what you're interested in, there's a day trip from Tokyo waiting for you. So, pack your bags, pick your adventure, and explore beyond the city lights!

CHAPTER 7

DISCOVERING KYOTO

Temples and Shrines

Kyoto, nicknamed the "City of Ten Thousand Shrines," is packed with stunning temples and shrines that hold deep historical and spiritual significance. They offer a peek into Japanese culture, religion, and artistry. Here are some top places to visit during your Kyoto trip:

Must-See Sights:

1. **Kiyomizu-dera Temple:**

Famous for its wooden stage hanging over a hillside, offering breathtaking views of the city.

2. **Kinkaku-ji (Golden Pavilion):** A Zen temple covered in gold leaf, reflecting in a serene pond.

3. **Fushimi Inari-taisha Shrine:** Known for its thousands of red torii gates winding up a mountain, dedicated to the god of rice.

4. **Ginkaku-ji (Silver Pavilion):** Though not silver, it embodies Zen beauty with tranquil gardens.

5. **Ryoan-ji Temple:** Renowned for its minimalist rock garden, inviting meditation on impermanence.

Hidden Gems:

1. **Ninna-ji Temple:** A serene UNESCO site with a five-storied pagoda and beautiful gardens.

2. **Kōdaiji Temple:** A tranquil Zen temple famous for its gardens, especially during autumn.

3. **Kamigamo Shrine and Shimogamo Shrine:** Ancient Shinto shrines nestled in lush forests, dedicated to water deities.

4. **Fushimi Momoyama Inaritaisha Shrine:**

Often overlooked, offering a quieter experience with torii gates leading up the mountainside.

Explore Further:

This list is just the beginning; Kyoto boasts over 1600 temples and 400 shrines. Venture beyond the popular spots to find hidden sanctuaries that resonate with you. Remember, visiting these places isn't just sightseeing; it's a chance to immerse yourself in Japanese culture and appreciate its spiritual traditions.

Traditional Culture

Kyoto, steeped in history and tradition, offers a captivating insight into Japanese culture's heart. Beyond its stunning temples and shrines, a vibrant array of traditional experiences awaits the curious traveler. Here are some ways to delve into the essence of Kyoto's cultural heritage:

Witnessing the Arts:

- **Gion District:** Take a stroll through the atmospheric Gion district, Kyoto's geisha culture hub. In the early evening, catch a glimpse of a maiko (apprentice geisha) on her way to an appointment, adding enchantment to the historic streets.

- **Geisha Performances:** Delve deeper into the world of geisha by attending a performance. Experience the grace and artistry of these performers as they entertain with traditional music, dance, and storytelling. Make sure to make reservations in advance as spots can fill up rapidly.

- **Tea Ceremony:** Immerse yourself in the serene and meditative Japanese tea ceremony. Learn about the meticulous steps involved in preparing and serving matcha tea, appreciate the beautiful teaware, and experience the tranquility associated with this tradition.

- **Kimono Rentals:** Dress in a traditional kimono and explore Kyoto's streets. Choose from a variety of vibrant colors and patterns, and let professional stylists help you achieve the perfect look. Walking through historical neighborhoods in a kimono offers a unique and interactive cultural experience.

Exploring Craftsmanship:

- **Nishiki Market:** Engage your senses at Nishiki Market, a lively food market filled with fresh seafood, local produce, and specialty shops. Watch skilled vendors prepare food and discover unique ingredients used in Japanese cuisine.

- **Traditional Crafts Workshops:** Kyoto is famous for its craftsmanship. Participate in workshops to learn about techniques behind traditional crafts like silk dyeing, porcelain painting, or calligraphy. Craft your own distinctive souvenir to bring back home.

Seasonal Celebrations:

- **Hanami (Cherry Blossom Viewing):** If visiting in spring, don't miss hanami. Witness the breathtaking cherry blossoms at locations like Philosopher's Path or Maruyama Park. Enjoy picnics beneath the blossoms and soak in the festive atmosphere.

- **Gion Matsuri:** Held annually in July, Gion Matsuri is one of Kyoto's most famous festivals. Experience the vibrant energy and elaborate floats adorned with traditional decorations, immersing yourself in the city's cultural heritage.

Tranquil Retreats:

- **Arashiyama Bamboo Grove:** Find serenity in the Arashiyama Bamboo Grove. Take a leisurely stroll along pathways lined with towering bamboo stalks, creating a magical and calming ambiance.

- **Ryokan Stays:** For an authentic cultural experience, stay in a ryokan, a traditional Japanese inn. Experience Japanese hospitality, dine on kaiseki meals served in your room, and relax in a tranquil setting with tatami flooring and futon bedding.

By incorporating these experiences into your Kyoto itinerary, you'll gain a deeper appreciation for the city's rich traditions and vibrant cultural scene. Wander through historic streets, engage with local artisans, and participate in time-honored practices to discover the true essence of Kyoto.

Kyoto's Culinary Delights

Kyoto, the cultural and historical heart of Japan, isn't just a visual delight but also a tantalizing journey for your taste buds. Beyond its majestic temples and tranquil gardens lies a culinary world bursting with tradition, fresh seasonal ingredients, and a unique approach to food. Here's a peek into Kyoto's delicious cuisine:

Must-Try Dishes:

- **Obanzai:** This is Kyoto's home cooking at its best, featuring a variety of small, seasonal dishes made with fresh, local ingredients like simmered vegetables, grilled fish, and pickled plums, all bursting with flavor.

- **Yudofu:** A simple yet exquisite dish, yudofu features tofu simmered in a flavorful kombu (kelp) dashi broth, offering a comforting and healthy meal enjoyed with grated ginger, scallions, and soy sauce.

- **Kaiseki:** Indulge in the artistry of kaiseki, a multi-course culinary masterpiece showcasing seasonal ingredients with stunning visual appeal and a focus on balanced flavors and textures.

- **Tempura:** Kyoto's twist on tempura features high-quality seasonal vegetables and seafood lightly battered and fried to crispy perfection, highlighting the natural flavors of the ingredients.

Sweet Treats:

- **Wagashi:**

Kyoto is famous for its wagashi, traditional Japanese sweets made with ingredients like red bean paste, rice flour, and seasonal fruits, offering a delightful taste of Japanese confections.

- **Matcha:** A haven for matcha lovers, Kyoto offers everything from ceremonial grade matcha tea to matcha-infused desserts and beverages, allowing you to indulge in the unique flavor of this vibrant green tea.

Unique Culinary Experiences:

- **Nishiki Market:** Dive into the vibrant atmosphere of Nishiki Market, where you can sample delicious street food, witness skilled vendors preparing fresh produce and seafood, and pick up unique ingredients to create your own Kyoto-inspired meals.

- **Vegetarian Options:** Explore Kyoto's flourishing vegetarian cuisine, known as shojin ryori, creatively prepared with plant-based ingredients for a delicious and healthy alternative.

- **Cooking Classes:** Unleash your inner chef with a Kyoto cooking class and learn the secrets behind traditional dishes like obanzai or tempura, gaining a deeper appreciation for Kyoto's culinary techniques and flavors.

Beyond the List:

This list only scratches the surface of Kyoto's culinary scene. From hidden ramen shops serving rich broths to cozy cafes offering delectable Kyoto vegetable dishes, there's something to delight every palate. Explore local restaurants, street food stalls, and hidden gems to truly experience Kyoto's unique and unforgettable food culture.

CHAPTER 8

ADVENTURES IN OSAKA

Osaka's Vibrant Scene

Osaka, Japan's second-largest metropolis, buzzes with a vibrant energy distinct from its more reserved counterpart, Kyoto. Often dubbed the "City of Merchants" or the "Nation's Kitchen," Osaka is home to a lively street food scene, a bustling nightlife, and a welcoming, down-to-earth atmosphere. Below is a glimpse into the electrifying energy awaiting you in Osaka:

Dotonbori & Namba: Immerse yourself in the dazzling spectacle of Dotonbori and Namba districts, filled with neon lights, towering billboards, and a contagious energy. Explore the lively Dotombori Canal lined with restaurants and street vendors, marvel at the iconic Glico

Running Man sign, and treat yourself to Osaka's famous street food.

Kuromon Market: Food lovers rejoice at Kuromon Market, also known as Osaka's Kitchen, a sensory paradise bursting with fresh seafood, local produce, and specialty shops. Sample delectable street food, witness live seafood auctions, and soak in the lively market atmosphere.

Shinsekai District: Transport yourself back in time to the Shinsekai district, built in the early 20th century with influences from New York and Paris. Explore the retro vibes, visit Tsutenkaku Tower for panoramic views, and indulge in local favorites like takoyaki and kushikatsu.

Universal Studios Japan: Thrill-seekers shouldn't miss Universal Studios Japan, offering exhilarating rides, themed zones like the Wizarding World of Harry Potter, and immersive entertainment experiences.

Dotombori River Cruises: Take a scenic Dotombori River Cruise for a unique perspective of Osaka. Glide along the canal at night, admire the dazzling lights, and capture picturesque views of the city's landmarks.

Beyond the Tourist Trail:

- **Hozenji Temple (Floating Garden):** Find tranquility amidst the urban bustle at Hozenji Temple, featuring a captivating moss garden designed to resemble a floating garden.

- **Tennoji Park:** Escape to nature in Osaka's largest park, Tennoji Park. Explore tranquil gardens, visit the Osaka City Museum of Art, or enjoy boating on the central pond.

- **Osaka Castle:** Step into history at Osaka Castle, a magnificent landmark dating back to the 16th century, offering insights into Japan's feudal past.

- **Umeda Skybuilding:**

Ascend to the top of Umeda Skybuilding for breathtaking panoramic views of Osaka's skyline from its unique floating garden observation deck.

Osaka's charm lies in its infectious energy, its love for good food and good times, and its welcoming atmosphere. Embrace the city's unique character, delve into its vibrant culture, and savor the delicious food scene that has earned Osaka its reputation as "The Nation's Kitchen."

Street Food Paradise

Osaka proudly holds the title of "Nation's Kitchen" in Japan, and its street food scene promises an unforgettable culinary adventure for every visitor. Let's take a look at the mouthwatering treats awaiting you on Osaka's bustling streets:

Osaka's Must-Try Street Food:

- **Takoyaki (Octopus Balls):** These bite-sized balls of batter are filled with diced octopus, tempura flakes, and green onion, topped with savory takoyaki sauce, mayonnaise, and bonito flakes for a burst of flavor.

- **Okonomiyaki (Savory Pancakes):** Enjoy customizable savory pancakes made with a batter base of flour, eggs, and shredded cabbage, grilled with your choice of toppings like meat, vegetables, and sauces.

- **Yakisoba (Stir-Fried Noodles):** Osaka's version of yakisoba features thick noodles stir-fried with meat, vegetables, and Worcestershire sauce-based sauce, topped with a fried egg, pickled ginger, and seaweed flakes.

- **Kushikatsu (Deep-Fried Skewers):** Bite-sized skewers of meat, seafood, and vegetables are breaded and deep-fried to crispy perfection, served with a dipping sauce for an irresistible finger food experience.

- **Nikuman (Steamed Buns):** These fluffy steamed buns are filled with savory pork or vegetables simmered in a flavorful broth, perfect for a quick snack or meal on the go.

Where to Find Osaka's Street Food:

- **Dotonbori & Namba:** Explore the vibrant streets lined with neon-lit vendors and restaurants along Dotombori Canal, offering a wide variety of street food options.

- **Kuromon Market:** Dive into Osaka's Kitchen at Kuromon Market, where you can sample fresh seafood skewers, takoyaki, and other delectable bites from various vendors.

- **Hidden Alleys (Yokocho):** Venture into the atmospheric alleys hidden throughout Osaka, where tiny restaurants and street vendors offer authentic street food experiences off the beaten path.

Beyond the Classics:

- **Tako Senbei (Grilled Octopus):** Thin slices of octopus grilled to crispy perfection, brushed with a sweet soy sauce glaze for a unique textural experience.

- **Ikayaki (Grilled Squid):** Whole squid grilled over charcoal and brushed with a savory sauce, offering a smoky flavor and tender texture.

- **Kakigori (Shaved Ice):** Cool off with refreshing shaved ice dessert topped with condensed milk, fruit syrups, and sweet azuki beans for a sweet summertime treat.

With its wide array of choices, welcoming atmosphere, and focus on delicious flavors, Osaka's street food scene is an adventure waiting to be savored. Embrace the vibrant energy, be adventurous with your palate, and relish in the unique and unforgettable flavors that Osaka has to offer.

Osaka Castle and Beyond

Osaka Castle, a majestic symbol of power and resilience, is undoubtedly a must-see on any Osaka itinerary. However, the dynamic city offers a plethora of experiences beyond its towering walls. Below is how you can craft a captivating day that blends history with thrilling rides, mouthwatering bites, and hidden gems:

Morning:

Visit Osaka Castle: Start your day by exploring Osaka Castle, a big and old fortress from many years ago. Walk around the castle and learn about the person who built it,

Toyotomi Hideyoshi. You can also go up to the top for a good view of the city.

Afternoon:

Go to Dotonbori & Namba: After the castle, head to Dotonbori and Namba. It's a busy area with lots of lights and food. Take a picture with the famous Glico Running Man sign and try some delicious street food like octopus balls or noodles. Don't forget to have some shaved ice to cool down!

Evening:

Optional: Visit Universal Studios Japan: If you like rides and movies, you can spend your evening at Universal Studios Japan. There are fun rides and themed areas based on movies like Harry Potter and Jurassic Park.

Or try this:

Visit Hozenji Temple & Take a Boat Ride: For a quieter evening, visit Hozenji Temple with its pretty garden. Then, take a boat ride along the river to see Osaka's lights at night.

Dinner:

Eat at Kuromon Market: Finish your day by having dinner at Kuromon Market. It's a big market with lots of fresh seafood and restaurants. You can try different kinds of food, like grilled seafood or pancakes cooked in front of you.

Nightlife:

Explore Dotonbori & Namba: After dinner, explore Dotonbori and Namba at night. There are many bars, restaurants, and karaoke places to enjoy. Feel the lively atmosphere of Osaka as you end your day.

CHAPTER 9

CULTURAL EXPERIENCES

Tea Ceremony

Certainly! The Japanese tea ceremony, known as chadō or sadō, which means "the way of tea," holds deep cultural significance in Japan. What you can expect are:

The Setting:

Tea Room: The tea ceremony usually happens in a specially designed room, often small and with tatami flooring. The design is simple, focusing on natural elements to create a calm and mindful atmosphere.

The Host:

Kimono-Clad Host: A trained host, typically dressed in a kimono, meticulously orchestrates the tea ceremony. They embody grace, hospitality, and attention to detail.

The Ceremony:

Ritualistic Steps: The tea ceremony follows a specific sequence of steps, each carrying symbolism and performed with precision. These steps involve preparing the tea utensils, whisking the matcha, and serving the tea to guests in a particular order.

The Guest's Role:

Respectful Participation: Guests are expected to participate respectfully, following etiquette for entering and leaving the tea room, handling the teacup, and appreciating the presentation.

The Significance:

Zen Influence: The tea ceremony is strongly influenced by Zen Buddhism, emphasizing mindfulness, respect, and harmony with nature. It encourages appreciating the present moment and finding beauty in simplicity.

Experiencing the Tea Ceremony:

Attending a formal tea ceremony can be time-consuming and costly, but there are ways to include this cultural activity in your trip:

Tea Ceremony Experience Classes: Many places offer short introductory tea ceremony experiences for tourists. These classes allow you to learn the basic principles, practice etiquette, and taste matcha tea in a more accessible setting.

Tea Houses: Some traditional tea houses welcome visitors without reservations. Here, you can enjoy a cup of matcha tea in a relaxed atmosphere, often accompanied by a small Japanese sweet.

Beyond the Ceremony:

Matcha Sweets & Treats: Matcha, the finely powdered green tea used in the ceremony, is a popular flavor in Japan. You can try matcha-infused desserts, drinks, or even ice cream to experience its unique taste.

Tea Shops & Supplies: Dive into the world of tea by visiting specialty tea shops. Explore various teas, learn about different grades and brewing methods, and maybe purchase a tea set or matcha powder to recreate the tea ceremony experience at home.

Whether you participate in a full ceremony or simply enjoy a cup of matcha, the Japanese tea ceremony provides insight into Japanese culture, tradition, and the pursuit of beauty and serenity in everyday life.

Sumo Wrestling

Sumo wrestling, a captivating fusion of sport, tradition, and ritual, stands as Japan's national sport. Here's a comprehensive guide to getting yourself lost in the world of sumo wrestling:

Understanding Sumo:

Objective: The goal in sumo is straightforward: a wrestler must either push their opponent out of the ring (dohyo) or force them to touch the ground with any body part other than their feet.

Wrestlers (Rikishi): Sumo wrestlers, known as rikishi, are renowned for their immense size and strength. They undergo rigorous training and adhere to a disciplined lifestyle.

Tournaments: Six grand sumo tournaments are held annually, with three in Tokyo (January, May, September), and one each in Osaka (March), Nagoya (July), and Fukuoka (November). Tickets are available online or at convenience stores in Japan, with prices varying based on seating category and tournament day.

Attending a Sumo Tournament:

Atmosphere: Witness the unique atmosphere of a sumo tournament, from the intricate pre-bout rituals to the electrifying clashes between wrestlers, all amidst the roar of the crowd.

Etiquette: Show respect by applauding when a winner is declared, but refrain from cheering for individual wrestlers. Also, avoid using flash photography during the ceremonial rituals.

Dress Code: While there's no strict dress code, opting for smart casual attire is advisable for the occasion.

Alternative Sumo Experiences:

Sumo Stables (Heya): Outside of tournament season, consider visiting a sumo stable (heya) to observe rikishi training and gain insight into their rigorous routines. Look online for information on stables offering public tours.

Sumo Museums: Explore several museums across Japan dedicated to sumo wrestling, where exhibits showcase artifacts, explain rules and rituals, and provide glimpses into the world of rikishi. The Japan Sumo Association Sumo Museum in Tokyo is a notable starting point.

Beyond the Ring:

Yagura (Sumo Wrestler Figurines): As a souvenir, consider purchasing a yagura, a traditional figurine depicting a sumo wrestler, available in various sizes and styles as a unique memento of your sumo experience.

Chanko Nabe: Sample chanko nabe, a hearty stew enjoyed by sumo wrestlers to maintain their physique. Although you might not train like a rikishi, you can savor this flavorful dish at select restaurants in Japan, featuring a mix of meat, seafood, vegetables, and broth.

Sumo wrestling offers a captivating glimpse into Japanese culture, tradition, and sporting prowess. Whether attending a tournament, exploring a sumo stable, or delving into its history, you're bound to develop a deeper appreciation for this distinctive sport.

Traditional Festivals

Japan is famous for its lively and deeply traditional festivals, known as matsuri. These events, held all year round across the country, provide an opportunity to dive into Japanese culture, witness breathtaking displays, and soak in the festive ambiance. Here's a peek at some of Japan's most renowned traditional festivals:

Spring:

Takayama Spring Festival (Mid-April, Takayama): This grand festival showcases two intricately decorated floats adorned with detailed carvings and puppets. Colorful parades featuring vibrant costumes and lively music make for a mesmerizing spectacle.

Summer:

Gion Matsuri (July, Kyoto): Among Japan's most iconic festivals, Gion Matsuri offers a month-long lineup of events. Experience the city's lively vibe with a procession of beautifully adorned floats (yamabo and hoko) during this historic celebration.

Nebuta Matsuri (Early August, Aomori): Held in Aomori, the Nebuta Matsuri features giant illuminated floats depicting legendary warriors and mythical creatures. These vibrant floats parade through the streets accompanied by spirited drumming and dancing.

Autumn:

Kishiwada Danjiri Matsuri (Mid-September, Kishiwada, Osaka): This exhilarating festival features elaborately decorated floats (danjiri) racing at high speeds through the streets. Feel the excitement as teams of men pull the massive floats in a thrilling competition.

Winter:

Sapporo Snow Festival (Early February, Sapporo): A globally renowned event, the Sapporo Snow Festival showcases impressive snow and ice sculptures. Marvel at towering structures, intricate details, and dazzling displays that transform the city into a magical winter wonderland.

Beyond the Big Names:

While these festivals are widely recognized, Japan hosts numerous local matsuri throughout the year. These celebrations often center around specific Shinto shrines or Buddhist temples, offering a more intimate and authentic cultural experience. Seek information about local matsuri at your hotel or tourist information center.

Festival Tips:

- **Plan Ahead:** Major festivals draw large crowds, so consider booking accommodation and transportation in advance.

- **Dress Comfortably:** Festivals may require standing or walking for long periods, so wear comfortable shoes and dress for the weather.

- **Respect the Culture:** Follow proper etiquette, avoiding loud noises or disruptive behavior during ceremonies.

- **Embrace the Experience:** Immerse yourself in the festive atmosphere by trying local food, watching traditional performances, and embracing the unique energy of each celebration.

Traditional festivals are a vital part of Japanese culture, showcasing history, art, and community spirit. So, include a festival or two in your plans and get ready to be captivated by the enchanting world of matsuri!

CHAPTER 10

SHOPPING AND SOUVENIRS

Popular Shopping Districts

Tokyo, a vast city, is a shopper's paradise with diverse districts catering to various tastes and budgets. Here's a quick guide to some of the most popular shopping areas:

Ginza (Luxury & High-End Brands): Ginza is famous for luxury shopping, featuring renowned designer boutiques, flagship stores of international brands, and elegant department stores like Mitsukoshi and Printemps Ginza. The main street boasts dazzling window displays and an abundance of luxury goods.

Shibuya (Trendy & Youth Fashion): Shibuya is a hotspot for trendsetters, offering a maze of streets filled with shops ranging from edgy streetwear to popular Japanese fashion brands. Don't miss the iconic Shibuya Crossing, known for its bustling pedestrian scramble.

Harajuku (Pop Culture & Vintage): Harajuku is vibrant and youthful, known for its kawaii (cute) fashion trends, quirky accessories, and cosplay paraphernalia along Takeshita Street. Explore backstreets for vintage stores and hidden gems.

Shinjuku (Electronics & Pop Culture): Shinjuku is a bustling district with Akihabara, the electronics hub, offering a plethora of electronics stores, anime shops, and manga outlets. Visit Bicqlo for electronics or Kinokuniya for manga.

Asakusa (Traditional Souvenirs & Crafts): Asakusa provides a glimpse into old Tokyo with Senso-ji Temple and its surroundings hosting shops selling traditional souvenirs and crafts like kimonos, tea sets, and ceramics.

This is just the tip of the iceberg; Tokyo boasts many more shopping areas waiting to be explored. So, put on your walking shoes, grab your shopping bags, and dive into Tokyo's retail therapy haven!

Unique Souvenirs to Buy

Beyond the usual keychains and fridge magnets, Osaka offers a treasure trove of unique and memorable souvenirs that capture the city's vibrant spirit and rich cultural heritage. Here are some ideas to bring a touch of Osaka back home:

Foodie Delights:

- **Osaka Mix:** Take a walk on the wild side with Osaka Mix, a pre-packaged snack mix that combines unexpected sweet and savory flavors. Expect a combination of crunchy textures and quirky ingredients like noodles, dried seafood, puffed corn, and even chocolate!

- **Takoyaki Keychain or Plushie:** These adorable keychains or plushies, shaped like the iconic octopus balls (takoyaki), are a cute and functional way to remember Osaka's street food scene.

- **KitKat Flavors:** Japan is famous for its unique KitKat flavors, and Osaka boasts its own regional specialties. Look for flavors like matcha, sake, or even edamame (soybeans) for a truly unique taste of the city.

Osaka Fashion & Fun:

- **Dotombori Zipper Pouch:** Showcase your love for Osaka's iconic Dotombori district with a vibrant zipper pouch featuring the neon lights and lively atmosphere of this popular area.

- **Osaka-Themed Handkerchief (Tenugui):** Tenugui are traditional Japanese hand towels made from thin cotton. Find one with an Osaka design, featuring the city's emblem or famous landmarks, for a stylish and practical souvenir.

- **Minions Osaka Merchandise:** Fans of the popular Minions franchise can find adorable

Osaka-themed Minions merchandise, a quirky and playful souvenir that combines Japanese culture with these beloved characters.

Traditional Crafts & Art:

- **Osaka Bezaiku Dolls:** These handcrafted dolls, made from leftover kimono fabric scraps, are a unique and sustainable souvenir. Each doll has its own personality and charm, capturing the spirit of Osaka's recycling and creative spirit.

- **Shusen Dyeing Chopsticks:** For a touch of elegance, consider a pair of chopsticks decorated with the beautiful Shusen dyeing technique, a traditional form of stencil dyeing practiced in Osaka.

- **Bunraku Puppet Play Mask Replica:** Bunraku is a traditional Japanese puppet theater originating in Osaka. A miniature replica of a Bunraku puppet mask, with its intricate details and expressive features, makes for a unique and cultural souvenir.

Remember: When considering food items as souvenirs, check customs regulations of your home country to ensure they are allowed for import.

These suggestions are just meant to ignite your creativity. As you explore Osaka's vibrant markets, shops, and hidden alleys, keep your eyes peeled for unique and interesting souvenirs that reflect your own personality and capture the special essence of your Osaka adventure!

Tax-Free Shopping Tips

Here are some tips to make the most of tax-free shopping in Osaka, Japan:

Eligibility:

- **Non-Resident Tourists:** Tax-free shopping is for non-resident tourists with a valid passport. Make sure your passport is stamped upon arrival to prove your tourist status.

Minimum Purchase Amount:

- **Threshold for Tax Exemption:** Depending on the item type, you'll need to spend a minimum amount at a single store on the same day. It's generally 5,000 yen for general items and between 5,000 yen and 500,000 yen for consumables.

The Tax-Free Process:

- **Two Methods:** You can either show your passport at purchase to get tax deducted upfront or pay the full price and claim a refund later at a designated counter within the store.

Keep Your Receipts & Purchases Sealed:

- **Proof of Purchase:** Hang onto your receipts for customs inspection upon departure.

- **Unopened Consumables:** Keep consumables sealed until you leave Japan to avoid issues at customs.

Customs Regulations:

- **Declare Duty-Free Goods:** Declare tax-exempt items as "Tax Refund Goods" at customs when leaving Japan and have your receipts ready for inspection.

Additional Tips:

- **Plan Your Shopping:** Know which stores offer tax-free shopping and their minimum purchase requirements.

- **Ask Questions:** If unsure, ask store staff for help with the tax-free process.

- **Carry Cash:** While some stores accept cards, having cash is a good backup plan.

By following these tips, you can shop tax-free in Osaka smoothly, saving money and enjoying your shopping spree!

CHAPTER 11

PRACTICAL TIPS AND RESOURCES

Language Basics

Some useful Japanese phrases and tips to help you during your trip to Osaka are:

Greetings:

- **Konnichiwa (こんにちは) [Kon-nee-chee-wa]:** Hello (good afternoon)

- **Ohayō gozaimasu (おはようございます) [O-ha-yo go-zai-masu]:** Good morning

- **Konbanwa (こんばんは) [Kon-ban-wa]:** Good evening

Useful Phrases:

- **Arigatō gozaimasu (ありがとうございます) [A-ri-ga-toh go-zai-masu]:** Thank you

- **Dōzo (どうぞ) [Do-zo]:** Please (used to offer something or to invite someone to go first)

- **Sumimasen (すみません) [Soo-mee-mah-sen]:** Excuse me

- **Hai (はい) [Hai]:** Yes

- **Iiē (いいえ) [Ee-eh]:** No

Numbers (1-10):

- **Ichi (一) [Ee-chee]:** One

- **Ni (二) [Ni]:** Two

- **San (三) [San]:** Three

- **Shi (四) [Shi]:** Four

- **Go (五) [Go]:** Five

- **Roku (六) [Ro-ku]:** Six

- **Nana (七) [Nana]:** Seven

- **Hachi (八) [Hachi]:** Eight

- **Kyu (九) [Kyu]:** Nine

- **Jū (十) [Juu]:** Ten

Basic Questions:

- **Do you speak English? -** *Eigo hanashimasu ka?* (英語話しますか)

- **How much is this? -** *Ikura desu ka?* (いくらですか)

- **Where is the bathroom? -** *Toire wa doko desu ka?* (トイレはどこですか)

- **Excuse me, can you help me?** - *Sumimasen, tasukete kudasai.* (すみません、助けてください)

Tips:

- **Pronunciation:** Japanese pronunciation is generally easier for English speakers. Consonants are similar to English, and vowels are pure.

- **Politeness:** Using polite phrases like "kudasai" and "arigatou gozaimasu" is valued.

- **Non-verbal communication:** Bowing or gesturing can help convey respect.

- **Translation Apps:** Consider using translation apps for complex situations.

Learning these basic phrases will enhance your experience in Osaka and make communication smoother. Enjoy your trip!

Cultural Etiquette

To ensure a respectful and enriching experience in Osaka, here's a quick guide to some essential cultural etiquette:

Greetings and Bowing:

- **Bowing:** A bow is a universal sign of respect in Japan. A slight nod for casual greetings, a deeper bow for showing respect to elders or superiors.

- **Handshakes:** While not as common as bowing, handshakes are acceptable in business settings. Use a firm but gentle grip, and initiate the handshake only if you're the most senior person.

In Public:

- **Talking Loudly:** Public places in Japan tend to be quieter. Avoid loud phone calls or boisterous conversations on public transportation or in restaurants.

- **Queues:** Queues are formed orderly in Japan. Line up patiently and avoid cutting in line.

- **Eating and Drinking on the Move:** While grabbing a quick bite on the go is becoming more common, especially in younger generations, it's generally considered more polite to eat and drink at restaurants or designated areas.

Table Manners:

- **Chopsticks:** Hold chopsticks correctly (not like skewers!) and avoid using them to gesture or point. Rest them on a chopstick rest when not in use.

- **Slurping Noodles:** Slurping noodles is considered acceptable and even encouraged, as it enhances the flavor.

- **Itadakimasu & Gochisōsamadeshita:** Say "Itadakimasu" (いただきます) before you start eating (it means "I receive") and "Gochisōsamadeshita" (ごちそうさまでした) after you finish (it means "Thank you for the meal").

At Temples and Shrines:

- **Dress Code:** Dress modestly, especially when visiting temples and shrines. Avoid sleeveless shirts, short shorts, or overly revealing clothing.

- **Purification Ritual:** Many temples and shrines have a washing station (temizuya) at the entrance. Perform the purification ritual by rinsing your hands and mouth with water using the provided ladles.

- **Respectful Behavior:** Maintain a quiet and respectful demeanor. Avoid loud talking or disruptive behavior.

Gifts:

- **Gift-Giving:** Receive gifts with both hands and say "ありがとうございます (Arigatō gozaimasu)". Open gifts later in private.

Tipping:

- **No Tipping:** Tipping is generally not expected in Japan. The bill usually includes all service charges.

General Tips:

- **Taking Off Shoes:** In many places, including temples, shrines, some restaurants, and traditional Japanese inns (ryokan), it's customary to take off your shoes. Look for designated areas to place them.

- **Public Transportation:** Give up your seat for elderly people, pregnant women, or passengers with small children.

- **Escalators:** Stand on the left side of the escalator in Osaka (opposite in some other cities like Tokyo).

By following these basic etiquette guidelines, you'll demonstrate respect for Japanese culture and ensure a smooth and enjoyable experience during your visit to Osaka. Remember, a little effort goes a long way!

Emergency Contacts

In case of emergencies in Osaka, Japan, some important contact numbers to remember are:

- **Police (Fire/Ambulance):** 110 (This is a free emergency number. You can dial it from any phone, even a payphone without inserting coins.)

- **Fire/Ambulance (Optional):** 119 (This is another way to call for emergency fire and ambulance services.)

- **Tourist Police:** 06-6268-8001 (This number can be helpful if you need assistance with a non-life-threatening situation, such as a lost passport or stolen belongings. English-speaking officers are available.)

Tips:

- **Save the Numbers:** Consider saving these emergency numbers in your phone's contacts list for easy access.

- **Write Them Down:** If you don't have a smartphone or prefer not to rely on it, write down the emergency numbers and keep them with you in case of need.

- **Learn Basic Phrases:** Knowing a few basic Japanese phrases, such as "Tasukete kudasai" (たすけてください) which means "Help me," can be helpful in an emergency situation.

Remember, it's always better to be safe than sorry. By having these emergency contacts readily available, you can ensure a worry-free and enjoyable trip to Osaka.

Japan Travel Guide   J.B TERRY

CHAPTER 12

CONCLUSION

Final Thoughts on Japan

Japan is a country where old and new mix together. Here's a synopsis of what makes it unique:

Culture: Japan has rich traditions. You can see amazing things like theater shows and tea ceremonies. There are also beautiful temples and gardens to explore. Don't miss the fun festivals with their colorful parades.

Food: Japanese food is a real treat. You can try tasty dishes like sushi, ramen, and sweets. They also have unique flavors of green tea.

Technology: Japan is super advanced. They have fast trains, cool gadgets, and even robots!

Nature: Japan's natural beauty is stunning. You can hike in the mountains, walk through bamboo forests, or relax on beautiful beaches. And seeing Mount Fuji is breathtaking.

Hospitality: People in Japan are really nice. They're polite and make you feel welcome wherever you go.

Adventure: Visiting Japan is like going on a big adventure. You get to learn new things, try new foods, and make memories that last a lifetime.

No matter what you like, Japan has something for you. So, get ready to explore and have fun in this amazing country!

Encouragement for Future Travelers

The world is an incredible book, and those who don't travel only read one page! Here's a shot of inspiration to get your wanderlust revving:

- **The World Awaits:** Our planet is brimming with diverse cultures, breathtaking landscapes, and unforgettable experiences. Every journey is a chance to learn, grow, and discover something new about yourself and the world around you.

- **Embrace the Unknown:** Step outside your comfort zone and embrace the unknown. The most rewarding travel experiences often come from venturing off the beaten path and encountering the unexpected.

- **Collect Memories, Not Things:** Travel is not about acquiring souvenirs; it's about collecting memories that will enrich your life. Focus on the experiences you'll have, the connections you'll make, and the stories you'll create.

- **Travel Makes You Humble:** Exploring different cultures fosters humility and understanding. You'll gain a deeper appreciation for your own life while recognizing the beauty and richness of other ways of living.

- **Invest in Yourself:** Travel is an investment in yourself. It broadens your perspective, challenges your assumptions, and sparks creativity. The knowledge and experiences you gain will stay with you indefinitely.

- **Start Somewhere, Anywhere:** Don't let anxieties or limitations hold you back. Start with a short trip close by or a destination that's been calling to you. Every adventure, big or small, is a step towards a world of discovery.

- **You Don't Need to Break the Bank:** Travel doesn't have to be expensive. There are countless ways to travel on a budget, from budget airlines and hostels to volunteering and house-sitting opportunities.

- **The Journey is Just as Important:** Remember, travel is not just about the destination; it's about the journey itself. Savor the moments, embrace the unexpected, and enjoy the process of getting there.

So, pack your bags with curiosity, an open mind, and a sense of adventure. The world is waiting to be explored, and the most amazing experiences are just beyond your doorstep. Start planning your next adventure, and get ready to write your own travel story!

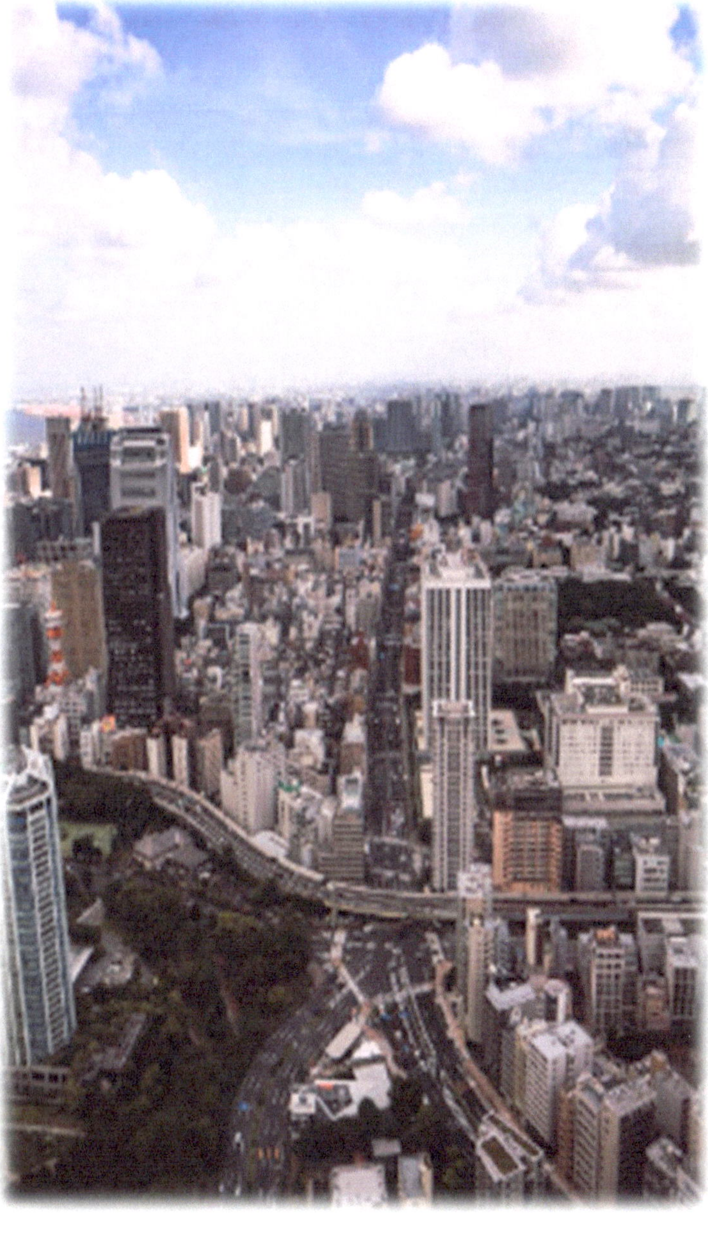

Chapter 13

Bonus section

Itinerary

Below is a suggested 10-day plan to explore Japan, covering popular spots and hidden gems. You can modify it to suit your plan:

Days 1-3: Tokyo Start in Tokyo, where you can visit iconic places like Shibuya Crossing and Sensō-ji Temple. Don't miss a tranquil stroll in the Imperial Palace East Garden. You can also take a day trip to Hakone for hot springs and scenic mountain views.

Day 4: Kamakura Take a day trip to Kamakura, known for its ancient temples and the Great Buddha of Kamakura.

Days 5-7: Kyoto Head to Kyoto to soak in its rich culture. Visit the Kiyomizu-dera Temple and explore the serene Arashiyama Bamboo Grove. Don't forget to take a day trip to Nara to see the tame deer in Nara Park.

Day 8: Hiroshima Learn about World War II history at the Hiroshima Peace Memorial Park and Museum.

Day 9: Miyajima Visit Miyajima Island to see the famous Itsukushima Shrine, which seems to float on water at high tide.

Day 10: Osaka End your trip in Osaka, known for its vibrant food scene. Try local delights like okonomiyaki and explore the bustling Dotombori district.

Remember, Japan has something for everyone, whether you're into history, nature, or food. When planning your trip, consider the best time to visit and budget accordingly. Japan is generally safe, but it's wise to stay aware of your surroundings. Pack weather-appropriate clothing, comfortable shoes, and consider learning a few basic Japanese phrases. Lastly, if you plan to travel extensively, getting a Japan Rail Pass can save you money on transportation. Most importantly, relax and enjoy your adventure!

Total Cost for A Trip to Japan

In addition to chapter 2, the total cost for a trip to Japan can vary based on several factors:

1. **Travel Dates:** Prices can fluctuate depending on whether you travel during peak season or shoulder seasons.

2. **Flight Costs:** Booking in advance, travel time, and your departure city can affect flight prices.

3. **Accommodation:** Options range from hostels and guesthouses to hotels and traditional ryokans, with prices varying accordingly.

4. **Transportation:** Consider the cost of a Japan Rail Pass for extensive travel within the country, as well as local transportation expenses.

5. **Food:** Budget for meals, which can range from street food to fine dining experiences.

6. **Activities:** Plan for expenses related to museum visits, temple admissions, tours, and other activities.

7. **Shopping:** Factor in any shopping you plan to do for souvenirs or personal items.

Here's an estimated cost breakdown for a 10-day trip:

- **Budget:** $1,500 - $3,000 USD
- **Mid-Range:** $3,000 - $5,000 USD
- **Luxury:** $5,000+ USD

Tips for Budget Travel:

- Opt for shoulder seasons to avoid peak prices.
- Consider alternative airports or off-peak flight times.
- Choose budget-friendly accommodations like hostels or guesthouses.
- Utilize a Japan Rail Pass for cost-effective travel.
- Make the most of Japan's efficient public transportation.
- Save on food expenses by enjoying street food and local eateries.

- Limit shopping or focus on affordable souvenirs.

For more information and assistance, refer to additional resources available to help plan your trip effectively.

The City Map

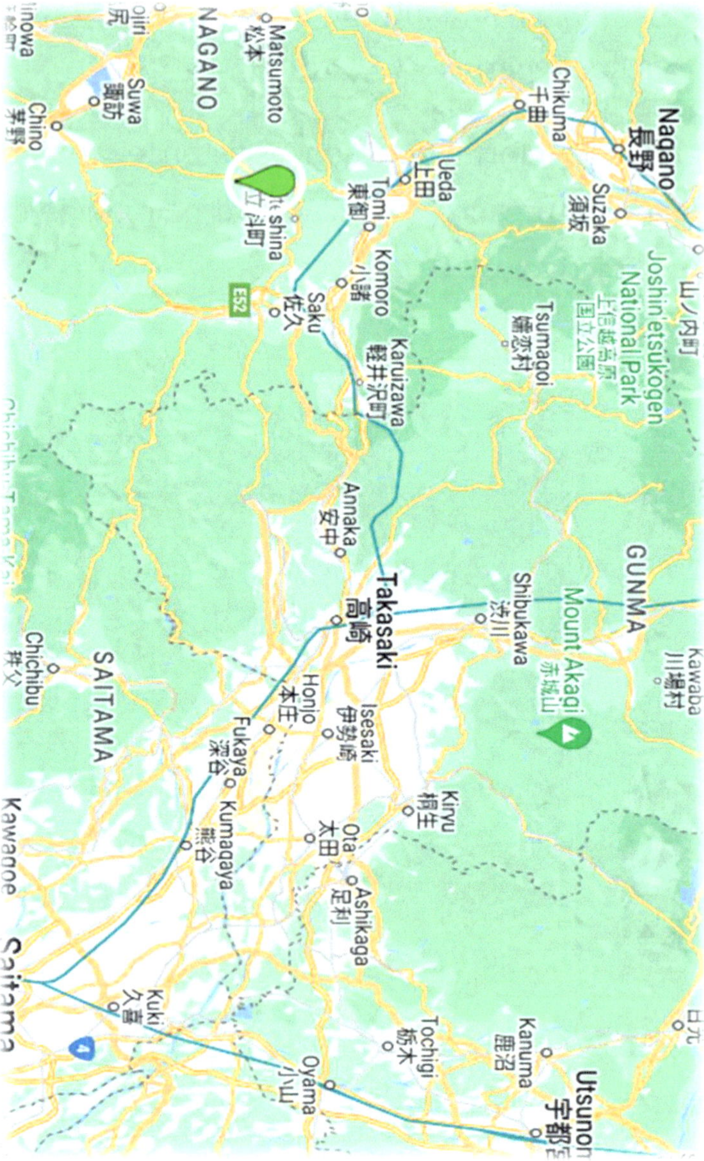
Nagano
長野
Chikuma
千曲
Suzaka
須坂
Ueda
上田
Tomi
東御
Komoro
小諸
Saku
佐久
Matsumoto
松本
NAGANO
Suwa
諏訪
Chino
茅野
E52
Joshin'etsukogen
National Park
上信越高原
国立公園
Tsumagoi
嬬恋村
Karuizawa
軽井沢町
Annaka
安中
Takasaki
高崎
GUNMA
Shibukawa
渋川
Mount Akagi
赤城山
Kawaba
川場村
Chichibu
秩父
SAITAMA
Honjo
本庄
Isesaki
伊勢崎
Fukaya
深谷
Kumagaya
熊谷
Kiryu
桐生
Ota
太田
Ashikaga
足利
Kawagoe
Saitama
Kuki
久喜
Tochigi
栃木
Kanuma
鹿沼
Oyama
小山

Travel Budget Planner

Travel Budget

Destination :

Travel Dates :

Details	Estimated	Actual
Accomodation		
Transportation		
Meals		
Activities		
Miscellaneous		

Notes

Travel Budget

Destination :

Travel Dates :

Details	Estimated	Actual
Accomodation		
Transportation		
Meals		
Activities		
Miscellaneous		

Notes

Travel Journals

TRAVEL JOURNAL
Weekly check in

DATE _____

TOP 3 PLACES TO VISIT THIS WEEK
1 _____
2 _____
3 _____

MOST REWARDING INTERACTION I HAD THIS WEEK
_____

THIS WEEK I FELT

NEXT WEEK I WANT TO _____

_____
_____
_____

THINGS I ACCOMPLISHED THIS WEEK
_____

THINGS I WILL LOVE TO SHARE WITH MY...
_____

MY RANKING OF THE WEEK
☆ ☆ ☆ ☆

161 | Japan Travel Guide   J.B TERRY

TRAVEL JOURNAL
Weekly check in

DATE _____

TOP 3 PLACES TO VISIT THIS WEEK
1 _____
2 _____
3 _____

MOST REWARDING INTERACTION I HAD THIS WEEK _____

THIS WEEK I FELT

NEXT WEEK I WANT TO _____

_____
_____
_____

THINGS I ACCOMPLISHED THIS WEEK _____

THINGS I WILL LOVE TO SHARE WITH MY... _____

MY RANKING OF THE WEEK
☆ ☆ ☆ ☆ ☆

TRAVEL JOURNAL
Weekly check in

DATE _____

TOP 3 PLACES TO VISIT THIS WEEK
1 _____
2 _____
3 _____

MOST REWARDING INTERACTION I HAD THIS WEEK _____

THIS WEEK I FELT

NEXT WEEK I WANT TO _____

_____
_____
_____
_____

THINGS I ACCOMPLISHED THIS WEEK

THINGS I WILL LOVE TO SHARE WITH MY... _____

MY RANKING OF THE WEEK

☆ ☆ ☆ ☆ ☆

Japan Travel Guide   J.B TERRY

TRAVEL JOURNAL
Weekly check in

DATE _____

TOP 3 PLACES TO VISIT THIS WEEK
1 _____
2 _____
3 _____

MOST REWARDING INTERACTION I HAD THIS WEEK
_____

THIS WEEK I FELT

NEXT WEEK I WANT TO _____

_____
_____
_____
_____

THINGS I ACCOMPLISHED THIS WEEK
_____

THINGS I WILL LOVE TO SHARE WITH MY...
_____

MY RANKING OF THE WEEK
☆ ☆ ☆ ☆ ☆

NOTES

Thank you for reading this travel guide. We hope that this guide has provided you with useful information for this your amazing and lasting memory to Japan. Whether you are interested in history, culture, or nature, Japan has something for everyone. We hope that you have a wonderful trip to Japan and enjoy all that this beautiful city has to offer.

Please, if you found this book helpful, please leave a positive review on its page. Your support fosters a community of learning.

Made in United States
Troutdale, OR
04/20/2024